THE WIND CARRIER

A COLLECTION OF POEMS

RUGMINI S RAJ

To Deepthy Raj

My Amma

Contents

Prologue   *vii*

  1. Who Am I   1

  2. This City Of My Childhood   3

  3. You And Me   5

  4. She   7

  5. The Secrets Held   9

  6. I Let Go Of Today   10

  7. Freedom   11

  8. Fleeting Glimpse   12

  9. Dawned In Death   14

10. Everyday   16

11. We Who Could Afford To Be Poor   18

12. Dear Country I Am Not The Strongest   20

13. Brewing Love   23

14. Dreams   24

15. The Women's Mind   25

Prologue

"Hope is the thing with feathers that perches in the soul — and sings the tunes without the words — and never stops at all."
— Emily Dickinson

1. Who Am I

Who am I they asked
And I don't know what to say
If they asked me, what am I?
I would have told them,
I am carbon,
I breathe and I grow
What am I?
A human being
But they asked me who am I?
Am I my age
Am I my dream
Am I what I am now
Am I those I love or those who love me
AlasI don't know
But when I pondered on,
In a sleepless night,
The question I left unanswered
Who am I?
Learned the part of the truth
Now I'll tell you what I learned
I am an ever-flowing river,
coursing through the lives of others—
I nurture in some places
and leave behind chaos in others.
I, I am not stationary.

Who am I they asked me,

And now I know partly the answer

I am always in motion,

both shaping and shaped by everything around me.

Living partly on my choice

and largely by the world's dictates

The world whose identity I mirror.

Am I selfish you ask me

Yes, I am selfish, yet selfless.

I will tell you one more thing

You know me as

I am everything one can see,

for I have been moulded by them all;

yet, you do not know me

As I am nothing,

I know just one thing that

I have nothing that is entirely my own.

Even My life is borrowed from death,

a gift from my parents,

and a mercy of this world.

I do not own the body I am.

Now you know who I am

If you don't, do not worry,

Cause now you know who I am not

2. This City of My Childhood

This city of my childhood
I spent my days and nights here,
Though I still live here
I now see little of her old self
Her old grace, her shining smile,
Had it all left her?
She has changed just like me
I left my childish innocence,
She left her peaceful soul.
My smiles and laughter that I lost,
In that time, she grew to bustle
The memories I shared with her
I lost them in a rush to live
I search for them now
In a land discovering herself
they say she has evolved
Maybe that's where her beauty lies
She grows to care for someone else
She is now someone else's joy
Now I, a lonely traveller in her
Alien to all that's there
The towering building, the fancy shops
I see none of the old
The dilapidated building of my past
Now shine with a fresh paint's coat
While she grew wiser and youthful
I grew melancholy and maybe wiser

I miss her old self,

But I know just enough to

Understand she is now someone else's friend

3. You and Me

You walk about with a smile
Your eyes they hold so much.
Oh, I hope I could save it but alas I am bound
You walk in with bandages to heal the wounds
You walk in with so much hope,
I can't tell that these need plasters, not bandages
If love had a face to me, it will be you
If forgiveness needed a mother
I know who that would be
I wish I could ease your pain
But pain is a weird thing,
it makes you scared
yet it makes you love those you hold close
Yes, I could save you,
But I am afraid
I am afraid I can't forgive like you,
I wish you didn't feel alone
in stitching together a cloth
A cloth tearing apart from the other side,
I wish I could tell you that your dream
does not have any place for me,
Cause I am scared of that dream,
I wish I could tell you that
you are mending what is already broken
I love you and more cause
you will always be a forgiver
I love you for you love what can't be loved easily

I love you cause you love
someone who is shattered and unyielding
Yes, you love me
and that is your greatest act of forgiveness
Mother you are always there,
an armour for me through my life
You are all I need,
yet I can't be a part of your dream

4. She

I saw her in the street
The merciless streets they are
She some fifteen or so
Just as me
No, she was not like me
Her eyes were wiser,
Her lips more sturdy
No, she was not me
Her eyes pierced me,
Those perfect black eyes,
I quivered,
Those beautiful eyes on mine
Hers lips demanded an answer
Her lips didn't tremble,
Didn't move but asked
How is it that life is unfair for me
I could have looked away,
No, I could not look away,
Cause she is me,
Born the same year,
Maybe the same day
Me in my uniform,
She in her own uniform
One of school, the other of injustice-
The barrier between us
She a fighter,
I a dreamer,

She a fighter who dares to dream
I a dreamer who can dare to fight
Now, we part ways
Me going to my home,
To my loved ones warm embrace
She to find a way in life
Probably seeking her next meal
We part, no words exchanged
No looks shared,
What would I tell her,
There was nothing to tell
Maybe she knew it too

5. The Secrets Held

Oh Rain, you are numerous
Not just in shape, but also in form,
various in style and more varied at your heart
You seem like you have so much to share
But so little time,
that you burst out every now and then
with tears of mirth and of pain
Rain, do you have secrets to tell,
cause l am ready to hear
I have dreams and hopes in me
and now I feel so do you
Is thunder your laughter or your sad heave
Is lightning your anger or your melancholy droop
Tell me rain, tell me
Are you looking for something on the earth,
is that why you wander here?
Or do you miss your home,
the place where you were born,
when you are high up there
Now you have gone again,
maybe to search some other,
or to find a better listener.
Somewhere else you will shower now
adieu rain, till we meet again,
go wander around that's what is best

6. I Let Go of Today

I let go of today
To fight with past
I let it go
To dream the future
Now I stand in no man's land,
I have no past,
I have no future
I let go of today
Now I have nowhere to go
Now I see what I lost
To change a time that is gone
Now I see what I missed
To make what I never knew
Now I have nowhere to go
Nothing to do
Nobody to see
I let go of today
Now I live without memories
Now I live with an unkind past
Now I live with an unyielding future
I wish I never let go of today

7. Freedom

The intangible Beauty of freedom
A diamond that it is, luring you
It's beauty, a construct of the world,
Hence more beautiful
It flows with grace through our veins
It's what we desire the most,
But when I pause and think,
What do I really mean by freedom?
Freedom is mine you say
But ain't my freedom a lie,
a polite way of saying that,
the reins of my life are with someone else.
If I was truly free, would I ponder its existence,
Would someone then have to grant me freedom
we are not given the right to breathe,
But we are given the right to freedom
If freedom is bestowed,
then are we not merely a slave to those,
who decide when my liberation should begin?
My freedom is not mine,
It's a construct of my mind,
It's provided to me by my people and my country
My world and my family
Freedom is my mine,
my freedom is all I have I will fight for it,
Cause it's a dream I can nurture

8. Fleeting Glimpse

My train rumbled on,
The vision of the world a daze
Her speed mounted,
My weary eyes caught only fleeting shapes
The passing of the trees, the land
The moving buildings and the dancing water
They flashed before my eyes; I gazed on
Then in a lush green land,
My tired eyes spotted a man,
In an island of paddy, he stood
Alone with his two bullocks
The paddy swayed,
The green trees around welcoming
But he, he stood under a barren beech tree
His body's weight against it,
His one foot resting on its weakened bark.
He knew this tree,
His hands caressed it,
Brimming eyes full of tenderness
They knew each other,
Like a man of nature knowing nature's children
Like a man whose youthful childhood was
Held and preserved by this wise tree
They stood close,
Friends meant to share joy and anguish
Friends of youth,
The tree of his hide and seeks

Maybe of his mid-day sleeps
Today a companion,
In labour and reality
Helping him wear
his clothes of adulthood
They were unbothered and unknown of me
My eyes held this precious picture
And my train flew past,
In a journey of fleeting glimpses

9. Dawned in Death

I met dawn in the dark
It was the most wonderful feeling,
The death, the feeling of nothing
I let death be my saviour
My armour from life
Now I can't let it go
And I don't want to
I am free for the first time
First time in a lifetime
As death meets me
Now I can't feel pain
Now I can't be haunted by past
Now I can't fight or care
I am freed
Oh, here is where freedom lies
I am dawning to liberation
I am liberated by death
I got the freedom,
Which the world denied me
They shred me for my religion
Those who swore to protect
Where those who put me down
Now I am somewhere where all are equal
My liberation began when my life ended
In life they killed each day
I fought each day like Ekalavya
Now I have no need to rise, I can rest

I have reached the end of my pain,

With the end of my breath,

Because those around me never cared

When I cried for help

Did you turn, no, I

was just another story

Another news in a land with many

So now I have to find solace at my end

You made my loss of life, my greatest gain

When politics lied and those I elected hated me

I found peace as you killed me

The power I gave you

The power we gave you,

Wielded against me

Today I see the truth with my death

Now it's all dawning bright and clear

10. Everyday

Every day we kill, for a god who said peace is on the way.

In the land of a man who embodies nonviolence everywhere,

there is violence and tears there

Hatred and sold-out media

Re told histories, newfound lies

And enemies based on religion

A land where the gods would flee

A land where the name of Ram is called

the virtuous man who left his righteous thrown

His name is called as violence is inflicted to yield a thrown

I am tired of these never-ending attacks,

I am tired of the brand-new jihads everyday

The blood is boiling inside all,

There is no peace

Is this what we are meant to be

A land where justice has breathed her last

And freedom has been imprisoned

Where are we going

Where will we reach

When our greatest enemy lies dead

Aurangzeb, sued for his crimes

Crimes from centuries agone

As the crimes of today lie piled up

No one cares

Who am I talking to, no one

Go on, burn down another

Hurt someone new

Create enemies in all
Remember just this
If someone ever needs the truth
I will tell you
If somebody needs to save the land
I will try till my last breath
That all I can do
To fight for what is still not lost
To unearth what is hidden
I will try till and fail

11. We Who could Afford to be Poor

We who could afford to be poor,
We walk because we choose to,
Not for the dearth of money,
But for leisurely time.
We who use the last of the grains,
Not for having none at our homes,
But for wanting to save.
You and me,

We who can afford to be poor.
With us exist those who can't,
Who live in pain,
Trapped in a cycle they never chose.

Those who can't afford to be poor,
poverty is suffering,
hunger is every day.
For those who cannot afford to be poor
Yet we say we share the same pain.
But do we even fathom the pain
We, who bargain for less,
Not out of need,
But for sport—
Bargaining with those who have none,

With those who can't afford to be poor,

Who need even the miserable prices.
Cause The misery at home is more pricey
They who let us be,
Because even the inadequate in necessary at home.
remember though

They have homes just like us,
And in that, we are all the same.
But we deny these dreams,
the real similarities.
We create thoughts where we are all the same—
In that one place where we are not
We deny that the world
Is more harsh on them,
And less so for us.

We deny that they sleep at night
With the same dreams as us.
We deny the truth
And live a lie.

Remember—
Though we all are the same,
They are in greater pain and need.
Not out of their mistakes,
But out of a world
That never helped them.
We are similar and dream alike.
It's we—Not us and them.

12. Dear Country I am Not the Strongest

I tried to shield you and be the armour
I tried to save you from the pain
I tried to be the rain to ease the pain
I am sorry but maybe I am not the strongest
I sought to grow the seeds of tomorrow
But I drowned in a sea of yesterday
I tried with my frail hands
To save you from being felled
but I am afraid I am not the strongest
I tried, but saved no plants of today
The hopes of today that they hold
In a room of fear, they withered down,
there I tried to grow a forest
but the land fertile once, now lay barren
I am sorry, I tried
I tried, to grow love, but saw pain
I tried, to protect, but saw despair
I tried, to nurture but saw disdain
They pierced through you
Stabbed your heart
They lied to you and me
They took your soul away from you, away from me
Now I see a forest fire of mistrust and hatred alight.
I tried to smother
But I feel I am not the strongest
They let you be drowned,

now there's a land I do not know

These children, the seeds of tomorrow,

Now laid down, scared

They uncared for, lay in darkness

I do not know what to do.

But I am afraid I am not the strongest

The pains that are wrought, how will I mend them.

I have no needle, l have no thread

You grew me up, now don't leave me.

Tell me how to grow back the seeds and the plants,

Tell me how to grow back the woods I knew

The land I knew, is now not mine

I am sorry I let you down

They took you away, For something else

A place I could never love

I want to save you

But know not how

I am just your seed from yesterday

Oh, my dear country,

My soil, my strength, you held me close

But now there is a drought of love,

in a sea of hate we live

I can't quench my thirst in this drought

But there is water everywhere

I tried my dearest country,

I tried to wipe the tears

I tried to plant hope

But I know I am not the strongest.

Forgive me,

I failed you

But I know not how to mend

I have no strength,
I am sorry but I am not the strongest

13. Brewing Love

I saw you in the midst,
crowd pushing us part.
You seemed welcoming, peaceful, calm.
I saw you look beautiful.
Warm and steamy.
I gazed at you,
I knew this love at first sight.
I tried to reach you.
But the crowd pulled me away from.
You had them all in your gaze.
It seems now that you are chiding me,
telling me I can't have you.
Now they call my name
and I take you from your tray.
After a day so hard,
I sipped into the steaming cup of chai,
my love at first sight

14. Dreams

Dreams are the most beautiful beings,
they walk in when they like,
leave when they face scorn.
Dreams are so varied
some walk away,
when we most need them,
The ones, that don't stay,
but we hold on close,
dreams that were never ours
Some stay, quiet and true,
Not always seen,
But the ones that really care
Then there are some dreams,
naughty ones, dreams luring us,
ones we desire the most,
maybe deserve the most,
but they are always in flight,
staying nowhere,
leaving us behind in despair
Dreams are all around,
as varied as us,
but then always there,
Unique and exciting.
Dreams, like us are never the same yet the same

15. The Women's Mind

The recollections I have are painful,
These memories are ghost
I try to keep from breaking
But I am failing
I know these ghosts are not the biggest
I know some have bigger ones,
Mine might even be trivial,
Yet I can't let them go
They haunt me like anabella.
They tell me sickly truths,
I want to run away but can't
They are all around,
Icy cold yet burning
What can I do? Nothing
oh save me
I have no one to heed to
I want to let go
But I can't cry,
Cause I have a family,
A family that lives to see me smile.
I can't break,
Cause i have an Amma i love,
Who let go all for my life
I can't hide away,
I have children to protect
I have promises to keep
I can't sleep,

i have a family to care for

I love them,

So I draw a smile,

A smile that is a farce

I feel a liar in me.

But I can't let love down,

So I hold on to the pain.

A storm rises in me,

I feel breathless,

I Break it, break it by smiling

My insincere feelings are getting me

They hurt cause now,

I am not true to myself

But I have no choice

So I go on